HAL•LEONARD VIOLIN PLAY-ALONG
WORSHIP FAVORITES

VOL. 59

AUDIO ACCESS INCLUDED

MW00528463

PLAYBACK+
Speed • Pitch • Balance • Loop

To access audio visit:
www.halleonard.com/mylibrary

Enter Code
1636-4741-2445-6688

Recorded and Produced by Larry Moore
Violin by Hua Jin

ISBN 978-1-4950-5030-5

HAL•LEONARD® CORPORATION
7777 W. BLUEMOUND RD. P.O. BOX 13819 MILWAUKEE, WI 53213

Visit Hal Leonard Online at
www.halleonard.com

CONTENTS

Amazing Grace
(My Chains Are Gone)

Words by John Newton
Traditional American Melody
Additional Words and Music by Chris Tomlin and Louie Giglio

Here I Am to Worship
(Light of the World)

Words and Music by Tim Hughes

Build Your Kingdom Here

Words and Music by Rend Collective

cresc.

f   dim.

mp

f

rit.

How Great Is Our God

**Words and Music by Chris Tomlin,
Jesse Reeves and Ed Cash**

Lead Me to the Cross

Words and Music by Brooke Ligertwood

Lord, I Need You

Words and Music by Jesse Reeves, Kristian Stanfill,
Matt Maher, Christy Nockels and Daniel Carson

10,000 Reasons
(Bless the Lord)

Words and Music by Jonas Myrin and Matt Redman

Sing to the King

Words and Music by Billy James Foote

Sacred Instrumental Collections
FROM
HAL LEONARD

HYMNS FOR THE MASTER
Book/CD Packs
15 inspirational favorites, including: All Hail the Power of Jesus' Name • Amazing Grace • Crown Him with Many Crowns • Joyful, Joyful We Adore Thee • This Is My Father's World • When I Survey the Wondrous Cross • and more.

00841136	Flute	$12.95
00841137	Clarinet	$12.95
00841138	Alto Sax	$12.95
00841139	Trumpet	$12.95
00841140	Trombone	$12.95
00841239	Piano Accomp. (No CD)	$8.95

PRAISE & WORSHIP HYMN SOLOS
Book/CD Packs
15 hymns arranged for solo performance by Stan Pethel. Includes: Blessed Be the Name • Come, Thou Fount of Every Blessing • Fairest Lord Jesus • My Faith Looks Up to Thee • To God Be the Glory • We Have Heard the Joyful Sound • more.

00841375	Alto Sax	$12.95
00841376	Clarinet/Tenor Sax	$12.95
00841378	F Horn	$12.95
00841373	Flute	$12.95
00841374	Piano Accompaniment	$8.95
00841379	Trombone/Baritone	$12.95
00841377	Trumpet	$12.95
00841380	Violin	$12.95

SOUNDS OF CELEBRATION
SOLOS WITH ENSEMBLE ARRANGEMENTS FOR TWO OR MORE PLAYERS
arr. Stan Pethel • Daybreak Music
Here's a new series useful to fill plenty of solo and ensemble needs. Whether it's a soloist using a book (accompanied by piano or the fully-orchestrated accompaniment track) or two, three, four players, or a full orchestra, *Sounds of Celebration* is a uniquely flexible new idea for church instrumentalists! Each book includes a solo line and an ensemble line. Mix and match lines with different instruments if used with an ensemble, or play the solo line when used as a solo book. Titles include: As the Deer • Give Thanks • He Is Exalted • Lord, I Lift Your Name on High • More Precious Than Silver • Shine, Jesus, Shine • Shout to the Lord • and more.

08742501	Conductor's Score (with Acc. CD)	$24.99
08742502	Flute	$5.95
08742503	Trumpet	$5.95
08742504	Clarinet	$5.99
08742505	Trombone	$5.95
08742506	Horn	$5.95
08742507	E♭ Alto Sax	$5.95
08742508	B♭ Tenor Sax	$5.95
08742509	Violin	$5.95
08742510	Cello	$5.95
08742511	Bass/Tuba	$5.95
08742512	Percussion 1, 2	$5.95
08742513	Piano/Rhythm	$9.99
08742514	Accompaniment CD	$26.99

HAL•LEONARD® CORPORATION
7777 W. BLUEMOUND RD. P.O. BOX 13819 MILWAUKEE, WI 53213
www.halleonard.com

Prices, contents and availability subject to change without notice.

SOUNDS OF CELEBRATION – VOLUME 2
SOLOS WITH ENSEMBLE ARRANGEMENTS FOR TWO OR MORE PLAYERS
arr. Stan Pethel • Daybreak Music
This sequel to the successful Volume One contains a wealth of popular praise choruses blended with favorite hymns. Perform with one, two, three, four or more players! Mix and match instruments regardless of your weekly attendance. Songs include: All Hail King Jesus • Find Us Faithful • Give Thanks • Be Glorified • Sanctuary • I Surrender All • Come Thou Fount • Now Thank We All Our God • and many more.

08743309	Conductor's Score	$24.99
08743310	Flute	$5.95
08743311	Trumpet	$5.95
08743312	Clarinet	$5.95
08743313	Trombone	$5.95
08743314	F Horn	$5.95
08743315	E♭ Alto Saxophone	$5.95
08743316	B♭ Tenor Saxophone	$5.95
08743317	Violin	$5.95
08743318	Cello	$5.95
08743319	Bass/Tuba	$5.95
08743320	Percussion	$5.95
08743321	Piano/Rhythm	$9.95
08743322	Accompaniment CD	$26.99

WORSHIP FAVORITES
Book/CD Packs
Features solo arrangements of 15 powerful and well-known songs. The full-accompaniment, play-along CD with tempo adjustment software lets solo instrumentalists sound just like the pros! Songs include: Agnus Dei • Great Is the Lord • He Is Exalted • Here I Am to Worship • In Christ Alone • Indescribable • Mighty to Save • There Is a Redeemer • The Wonderful Cross • and more.

00842501	Flute	$12.99
00842502	Clarinet	$12.99
00842503	Alto Sax	$12.99
00842504	Tenor Sax	$12.99
00842505	Trumpet	$12.99
00842506	Horn	$12.99
00842507	Trombone	$12.99
00842508	Violin	$12.99
00842509	Viola	$12.99
00842510	Cello	$12.99

WORSHIP SOLOS
Book/CD Packs
These book/CD packs let solo instrumentalists play with great-sounding full-band accompaniment tracks to 11 classic worship songs: Ancient of Days • Come, Now Is the Time to Worship • Draw Me Close • Firm Foundation • I Could Sing of Your Love Forever • My Life Is in You, Lord • Open the Eyes of My Heart • The Potter's Hand • Shout to the Lord • Shout to the North • We Fall Down.

00841836	Flute	$12.95
00841840	Tenor Sax	$12.95
00841841	Trumpet	$12.95
00841843	Trombone	$12.95
00841844	Violin	$12.95
00841846	Cello	$12.95
00841847	Piano Accompaniment for Winds (No CD)	$8.95
00841848	Piano Accompaniment for Strings (No CD)	$8.95